MUSIC SINCE 1939

£3

269 2

THE ARTS IN BRITAIN: NO. 7

The late Sir Henry Wood conducting one of his Promenade Concerts
at the Royal Albert Hall, London

MUSIC SINCE 1939

By

ROLLO H. MYERS

Illustrated

Published for

THE BRITISH COUNCIL
by LONGMANS GREEN & CO
LONDON   NEW YORK   TORONTO

LONGMANS, GREEN AND CO. LTD.
6 & 7 CLIFFORD STREET, LONDON, W.1
NICOL ROAD, BOMBAY, 1
17 CHITTARANJAN AVENUE, CALCUTTA, 13
36A MOUNT ROAD, MADRAS, 2

LONGMANS, GREEN AND CO. INC.
55 FIFTH AVENUE, NEW YORK, 3

LONGMANS, GREEN AND CO.
215 VICTORIA STREET, TORONTO, 1

LONGMANS' CODE NUMBER: 10039

THIS BOOKLET IS PRODUCED IN
COMPLETE CONFORMITY WITH THE
AUTHORISED ECONOMY STANDARDS

BRITISH COUNCIL'S CODE NAME: ART (MUSIC)

First published 1947

SET IN MONOTYPE PERPETUA
DESIGNED BY ERIC GILL

PRINTED IN GREAT BRITAIN
BY R. & R. CLARK, LIMITED, EDINBURGH

CONTENTS

ILLUSTRATIONS

MUSIC SINCE 1939

I. MUSICIANS IN BATTLE-DRESS

On the outbreak of war in September 1939 music in Britain was in a flourishing state. The London Music Festival held in May had been widely attended by visitors from all parts of the world, and was dominated by the presence of Toscanini who had conducted a brilliantly successful series of concerts given by the B.B.C. Symphony Orchestra in the Queen's Hall. All over the country people were taking an ever-increasing interest in music; high-class concerts were attracting large audiences in all the leading towns; and the programmes broadcast by the B.B.C. were creating a new public for music in every corner of the British Isles. British composers, too, were by now not only established firmly in the esteem of music-lovers at home; they were receiving for the first time in foreign countries the recognition that was their due. In a word, the musical horizon in Britain was clear, and the barometer pointed unmistakably to a long period of " set fair ".

But with the dropping of the first German bombs on Poland on 1st September 1939 conditions changed over-night. A blow had been struck at the very foundations of peace, brutally interrupting that international harmony so essential for the healthy development of universal culture. In England musicians were the first to suffer. Uncertainty as to the future and fears of immediate bombing dislocated professional life in every branch. Artists had their contracts cancelled; concert-giving organisations were unable to lay their plans; and most composers found it impossible to proceed, for the time being, with work in progress. Evacuation and dispersal were the order of the day, and all this led to a suspension of musical activities, which, however regrettable, could hardly have been avoided.

Gradually, however, as the first months of the " phoney " war wore on, it became possible to take stock of the situation, and soon tentative attempts were made in various ways to get music started again and organised on a war-time footing. It must be admitted that the music programmes broadcast by the B.B.C. in the early months of the war erred on the side of timidity, preference being given to the banal and ultra-familiar, with an excessive amount of programme time devoted to the broadcasting of commercial gramophone records. It must be borne in mind, however, that the principal broadcasting orchestras and programme staffs were evacuated to their war-time bases as soon as hostilities were declared, and this naturally entailed a considerable amount of administrative readjustment. Military service also claimed a considerable percentage of orchestral personnel throughout the country; and this of course affected every branch of the musical profession, which lost to one or other of the Services a number of gifted musicians of both sexes. In due course, however, many of our leading executants were drafted into specially constituted Service orchestras, chief among which was the Symphony Orchestra of the Royal Air Force (Director, Wing-Commander R. P. O'Donnell), which absorbed a large percentage of our best string and wind players, and did much to keep the flag of music flying wherever Service men and women were congregated in camps and training centres all over the British Isles.

C.E.M.A.

The year 1940 also saw the foundation of two institutions which played a very important part during the war years in keeping music alive and rendering it accessible to vast numbers of people, war workers of all kinds, and members of the Armed Forces. These were C.E.M.A. (Council for the Encouragement of Music and the Arts) and E.N.S.A. (National Service Entertainments Association). C.E.M.A. was started in June 1940 with a financial grant from the Pilgrim Trust and from the Treasury, while E.N.S.A., which catered more especially for the entertainment of the troops, came on the scene in October of the same year. Both these bodies organised concerts in air-raid shelters, factories, canteens and rest centres throughout the worst period of the Luftwaffe's offensive against this country, and the valuable work done by singers and instrumentalists who risked their lives during the heaviest raids " to bring the comforts and solace of fine music to those who were homeless and stricken" (to quote the words of Dr. Reginald Jacques, at that time musical Director of C.E.M.A.) is beyond all praise. It can truly be said that musicians were in the front line all through the war, because not only did they carry on in England during the various bombardments, but they also went overseas under the auspices of E.N.S.A. to give concerts to the troops on every front from Alamein to Burma.

C.E.M.A. (now known as the "Arts Council of Great Britain" or "Arts Council"), under the chairmanship of the late Lord Keynes, besides organising concerts with its own artists, many of which were (and still are) regularly broadcast, also gave financial support to Symphony Orchestras and Music Clubs in the form of guarantees against loss, and acted as agent for concerts arranged by the British Council for American troops, or by the Y.M.C.A. (Young Men's Christian Association) for British Forces in their camps and training centres. It also sponsored concerts for troops given by the B.B.C. Symphony Orchestra and other leading orchestras, and one of its most successful and interesting ventures was the organising of concerts of string music given in old and historic buildings in provincial towns. In all these activities C.E.M.A. had the expert guidance and support of a Music Advisory Panel consisting of well-known musicians, composers, performers and conductors. Some idea of the work accomplished may be gained from the following figures for one year only (1944) : the Hallé Orchestra of Manchester, the Liverpool Philharmonic and the London Philharmonic provided between them no less than 722 concerts to audiences totalling over a million; while the approximate amounts paid by Chamber Music Clubs associated with C.E.M.A. in fees to professional artists rose from £800 in 1941 to £7,500 in 1944.

E.N.S.A.

The work of E.N.S.A. lay chiefly in the direction of bringing entertainment to British and American troops both at home and abroad—work which entailed sacrifices on the part of artists and all concerned, faced as they were with the difficulties of war-time travel and of giving concerts under conditions which were often far from easy or agreeable. For example, eight concerts for troops and war workers in one day, ranging from the Isle of Wight to Belfast, was a by no means rare occurrence; and to these activities at home must be added the regular provision of music to our troops on all the fronts overseas and in stations in the Middle and Far East, such as Gibraltar, Malta, Cairo, Palestine, India and Burma. In 1943 a new experiment was tried in the form of a series of symphony concerts given by the B.B.C. Symphony Orchestra for men of the Army and Navy in their barracks at Aldershot and Portsmouth. The programmes of these concerts included not only classical works such as symphonies and concertos by Mozart and Brahms, and songs by Schubert, Wolf and Grieg, but also modern compositions by Walton, Bax and Sibelius; and although many of the men were hearing this type of music for the first time, they listened with concentrated attention and expressed their appreciation in the most enthusiastic manner. Naturally not all the music provided by E.N.S.A. was up to this standard, but the experiment showed that the most unlikely audiences will appreciate good music if given the chance of hearing it.

L.P.O. Tours

Indeed, one of the most remarkable features of musical life in Britain during the war was the quite phenomenal rise in popularity of symphonic music, which was made accessible to and enjoyed by sections of the community,—soldiers, sailors, airmen, factory workers, etc.—who up till then had shown little signs of appreciating classical music—perhaps from lack of opportunities. This phenomenon was especially noticeable among the inhabitants of some of the smaller provincial towns; and when the London Philharmonic Orchestra, conducted by Dr. Malcolm Sargent, made history by going on tour, in 1940, and playing to working-class audiences in a number of industrial towns in the Midlands and North of England, they were received with such enthusiasm that the small theatres and music-halls and cinemas, which often had to do duty for non-existent concert-halls, were packed to overflowing night after night. Symphonic music henceforth was accepted by the workers and ceased from then on to be the prerogative of a musical *élite*. The story is worth telling, for it is typical of a phenomenon (namely a most remarkable and ever-increasing appetite for good music amongst the people of Great Britain) which seems to have been directly stimulated by the war. The orchestra's tour was not, however, carried out in conditions of comfort and security, for it had scarcely started (this was in August 1940) when the Luftwaffe's raids on Southern England began, and soon spread to towns in the North and Midlands which were to be included in the tour. And yet throughout the whole period, in spite of the dislocation of communications, travelling difficulties, and all the dangers and discomforts of concert-giving under fire, not one member of the orchestra was injured, and not a single concert was cancelled. It was not until the orchestra was safely back in London that they had to face what was a major calamity—the destruction by enemy action in the spring of 1941 of London's principal and favourite concert-hall, known to musicians all over the world, Queen's Hall, Langham Place, W.1. The original home of the " Promenade " and Symphony Concerts, with which the name of Sir Henry Wood will always be associated, and the scene of some of the greatest triumphs of conductors of world-wide repute—Toscanini, Beecham, Nikisch, Kussevitzky, Bruno Walter, Monteux, Weingartner and many others —Queen's Hall was, in fact, the hub and focal point of the musical life of the capital. Its loss, as can readily be imagined, was therefore a most serious blow not only to the musical profession but to music-lovers everywhere.

As it happened, the London Philharmonic Orchestra was due to play there on the day following the air raid which destroyed the hall. But when the players arrived in the morning for the final rehearsal they found nothing but a burnt-out shell. To make matters worse a number of valuable instruments belonging to the musicians, which had been left at the hall over-night, had perished in the ruins, and for a time consternation reigned. But a spirit of defiance had been kindled, and in spite of everything another hall was found, and the concert took place as advertised. Instruments were borrowed from more fortunate musicians and from well-wishers, and soon the orchestra was facing life afresh. And from that day to this it has not looked back, giving concerts regularly, both in London and the provinces, and helping to keep up the high standard of orchestral playing which it shares with other leading British orchestras. It is interesting to note that the orchestra is self-supporting and managed by a committee drawn largely from the members. Before leaving the subject of the London Philharmonic, mention should be made of its founder and chief conductor, Sir Thomas Beecham. The adventures and vicissitudes outlined above were experienced by the orchestra during the early years of the war in the absence of their chief, who had had to leave England to fulfil engagements in Australia and elsewhere in the autumn of 1939. Among the many well-known conductors who conducted the London Philharmonic Orchestra during his absence may be mentioned Sir Adrian Boult, Mr. Basil Cameron, Mr. Anatol Fistoulari and Dr. Malcolm Sargent, while since the liberation of France the orchestra has been privileged to play under the *bâton* of both M. Charles Munch and M. Paul Paray. Sir Thomas now conducts the newly formed orchestra of the Royal Philharmonic Society.

It is of course impossible in the space at our disposal to do full justice to all the orchestras and musical organisations which continued to function and serve the cause of music during the war; omission of any names must therefore not be taken to imply a failure to recognise the value of the good work done by all. Consequently if we cannot do more than pay an undeservedly brief tribute to the work of such distinguished bodies as the London Symphony Orchestra (one of London's oldest and best-known orchestras) and the National Symphony Orchestra, created during the war, both of which have been fully engaged in performing the best symphonic music to eager and appreciative audiences, lack of space must be our only excuse.

It would not be fair, however, to omit a special reference to the fine work of the leading orchestras in the provinces—Manchester's famous " Hallé ", the Liverpool Philharmonic, the Scottish Orchestra of Glasgow and City of Birmingham Orchestra. The latter has been reconstituted since the war, and under its present conductor, George Weldon, has shown itself to be of excellent quality. The Liverpool Philharmonic, under its principal conductor, Dr. Malcolm

A concert organised by C.E.M.A. in the village church at Thaxted, Essex

Queen's Hall, the first home of the "Proms", seen through the Orchestra room, after its destruction by enemy action in 1941

Sargent, ranks high among British orchestras, and its programmes reflect the enlightened policy of the Philharmonic Society of Liverpool, which is the second oldest music society in the country, the oldest, of course, being the Royal Philharmonic Society of London—the Society which commissioned Beethoven to write his Ninth Symphony. The orchestra carried on throughout the war, giving hundreds of concerts, including some for children and for members of the Forces. It also made recordings, some of which were sponsored by the British Council—*e.g.* " Belshazzar's Feast ", by William Walton, with the Huddersfield Choir (one of Britain's best choral ensembles), conducted by the composer; the Arthur Bliss Piano Concerto with Solomon as soloist and Sir Adrian Boult conducting; Gustav Holst's " Hymn of Jesus ", and Elgar's " Dream of Gerontius ".

The record of the famous Hallé Orchestra, which has its home in Manchester, and is one of the oldest orchestras in the country, having been in existence for eighty-seven years, is also an impressive one. It now enjoys the privilege of playing regularly under the *bâton* of John Barbirolli, who has made it one of the finest orchestras in the country. The Hallé in 1944 gave 260 concerts all over the country in eleven months, and also paid a visit to France, Belgium and Holland where, under rigorous war conditions, it gave concerts to the British Liberation Army. During the blitz, when Manchester was the target for some of the fiercest attacks by the Luftwaffe, the Hallé Orchestra was deprived of its concert-hall, the Free Trade Hall, which was destroyed by bombs. The full story of the contribution made during the war by these fine orchestras cannot be related in these pages; but the inhabitants of these great industrial towns of the North are justly proud of their achievements, and have been generous in giving them unfailing support and encouragement throughout a period fraught with dangers and difficulties of every kind.

The " Proms "

A story which has to be told, however, is that of how the war affected the famous Promenade Concerts. These were the special creation of the late Sir Henry Wood, the great conductor, who died in his seventy-sixth year in the summer of 1944, only a few days before the conclusion of the fiftieth season of the " Proms ", which he had conducted almost without a break since their foundation in 1895.   By his death British music sustained a serious and irreparable loss; and although the " Proms " continue under other conductors, they are still, and always will be, known as " The Henry Wood Promenade Concerts ".   The debt owed by British music and musicians to this remarkable man cannot be over-estimated.   In the course of his fifty years of conducting it has been estimated that 75 per cent of all the orchestral music by established native composers was given under his direction.   Sir Henry, in the words of Sir Arnold Bax, which would certainly be endorsed by every other British composer of equal or lesser eminence, " has been esteemed a national institution. . . . He has purified and enriched the musical taste of at least two generations.   He has improved the quality of orchestral playing out of all knowledge; and we who enjoy the high privilege of his friendship . . . must feel it an honour to have lived contemporaneously with a great man who commands not only our deepest respect and admiration but also our unqualified affection."

A tribute such as the above coming from a composer as eminent as Sir Arnold Bax serves to show with what high esteem the late Sir Henry Wood was regarded among musicians; while his faithful and enormous public worshipped him with a fervour not far removed from adoration.

A word of explanation as to the exact nature of the Promenade Concerts associated with his name should perhaps be inserted here for the benefit of any readers who may not have a clear picture in their minds of the way in which these concerts, so peculiarly a British institution, are organised.   Very briefly the " Proms " (as they are invariably known and referred to in this country) are a series of orchestral concerts given nightly on six days of the week over a period of eight or nine weeks during the summer months. They are called " Promenade " concerts because a large proportion of the audience listens to the music standing up, the seats on the floor of the house having been removed for this purpose.   In this way the capacity of the hall is increased, which enables the price of

Basil Cameron conducting the London Symphony Orchestra at a Promenade Concert

Sir Adrian Boult, with Paul Beard, leader of the B.B.C. Symphony Orchestra, and Marie Wilson, former first violinist

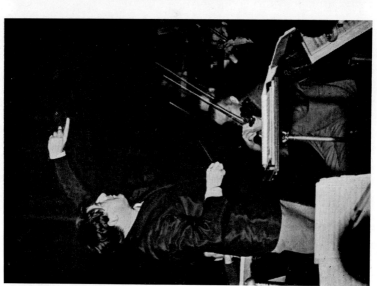

John Barbirolli, the conductor of the Hallé Orchestra

admission to the " Promenade " to be fixed at so modest a figure as to bring these concerts within the reach of the humblest purse. But for this small expenditure (there are, of course, higher-priced seats which can be reserved) it is possible for the musical amateur to hear in one season practically the whole classical repertoire of symphonic music, with a reasonably high proportion of new contemporary works thrown in. In addition, the best soloists, singers and instrumentalists are engaged, while the programmes throughout the long season are invariably executed by our leading orchestras under the direction, since the death of Sir Henry Wood, of conductors of established repute. For many years now these concerts have been sponsored by the B.B.C., and broadcast, either wholly or in part, so that the music performed can be heard by unseen audiences vaster than those which nightly throng the hall in London where the " Proms " are given.

That, then, is the picture. Let us take our minds back now to the night of Friday 1st September 1939. On that date the " Proms " had been running for three weeks. The orchestra engaged was the B.B.C. Symphony Orchestra. It had been arranged that, should war break out, the B.B.C. Orchestra would immediately, for security reasons, be evacuated to the country; this was merely a part of the complicated procedure to be adopted, on a signal from the Government, by the Corporation, which from that moment would be working to a pre-arranged emergency war-time schedule. Although Poland had been invaded in the early hours of the morning, the orchestra turned up as usual for rehearsal, but no one then knew whether the Promenade Concert would take place that evening. The decision was finally taken to carry on; but that was to be the last concert of that ill-fated season. The audience on leaving the hall found themselves engulfed in the first total " black-out " of the war—a black-out which was to be maintained for over five long years —and the next day the B.B.C. Symphony Orchestra had left London for its war-time base.

But the " Proms " were not dead. The following year—1940— they were held again, although the last concert of the season was brought to a sudden end by one of the Luftwaffe's fiercest raids on London. Before the 1941 season was due to begin the Queen's

Hall, the original home of the "Proms", had been destroyed, as
already related, so a new home for them was found in the much
larger but less suitable Albert Hall in Kensington ; and there they
have been ever since. Public support for these concerts showed
no falling off, and audiences of 4000 to 5000 a night were by no
means uncommon. Sir Henry Wood, true to his lifelong practice
of encouraging contemporary music, continued to bring out new
works, and in two seasons (1942–1943) no fewer than 42 works
received their first performance in England at these concerts. In
the summer of 1944, however, attacks by the V1 weapon—the
flying bomb—began, and once more the "Proms" had to be interrupted. Those scheduled to be broadcast were performed in the
studio, but the public concerts had to be discontinued. This was a
great disappointment to all concerned as the season was the fiftieth
to be conducted by Sir Henry, and if carried to its conclusion would
have been the crowning triumph of the veteran conductor's career.
The fates, however, decreed otherwise, and Sir Henry, who had for
some time been in failing health, was struck down by a fatal illness
and died just before the last concert of the season, which it was hoped
he would be able to conduct himself, was broadcast from a studio
in the country at the B.B.C. Symphony Orchestra's war-time base.
Thus ended an historic chapter in the annals of British music. The
"Proms", it is true, continue, but their founder and creator is no
more, although his spirit still animates the work of his successors,
and lives on in the affection of the public he created.

National Gallery Concerts

Looking back at the long grim years of war during which these
islands were beleaguered and cut off from all contact with the
continent of Europe—years of total black-out in town and country,
of rationing and privations of every kind, of long hours of work and
difficulties of transport and communications—it is not surprising
that the people of Britain, harassed and uncertain as to their fate,
should have sought solace in almost the only art that was able to
survive these perilous conditions—music. For it must be remem-
bered that for long periods theatres and most places of amusement

were forced to close their doors, while picture galleries and museums had been emptied of their previous contents early in the war as a precaution against air attack.　Music, however, was mobile; and musicians were not slow to see in what way they could best serve their country.　At first improvisation was the order of the day, although later on, as we have seen, the musical life of the country was pretty well organised to meet the abnormal conditions imposed by the war.　But a start had to be made, and it is a comforting reflection that every appeal, whether to artists to come forward and co-operate, or to the public to lend their support, invariably met with an eager and enthusiastic response.

One of the earliest musical ventures of the war, which in the long run proved as successful as any, surviving for a time the change-over from war to peace, was the organisation of the National Gallery Concerts.　The idea was conceived by one of Britain's most distinguished pianists, Dame Myra Hess, who felt very strongly that one of the best ways to satisfy the public's need for mental refreshment and relaxation in the early days of the war, when all theatres, cinemas and concert-halls in London had been shut by order of the Government, would be to provide chamber-music concerts of short duration, but of high quality, daily for the benefit of war workers during their lunch hour.　The question was: Where could these concerts take place? Someone suggested the National Gallery in Trafalgar Square, which was then standing empty, all the pictures having long since been evacuated to safe hide-outs in the country.　On being approached, the Director, then Sir Kenneth Clark, gave his enthusiastic support to the scheme, and within a very short time permission had been obtained from the Government to use the Gallery; a committee was set up, and the first concert took place on 10th October 1939. This took the form of a piano recital given by Myra Hess, and the public's response was immediate and most encouraging.　The price of admission was fixed at the nominal figure of one shilling, which was maintained throughout, and the very first concert was heard by an audience of 1000 people.　During the daylight bombing of London in the autumn of 1940 it was necessary to hold the concerts in one of the Gallery's basement shelters, and the building was hit by bombs on more than one occasion.　When it was necessary to evacuate, the concerts were not interrupted: they merely took place in another building. On one occasion an unexploded bomb went off in the Gallery while a concert was in progress; but no one in the audience moved, and the Stratton String Quartet continued their performance of Beethoven's F major " Rasoumovsky " quartet without missing a beat.

An enormous number of works, new and old, has been performed at these concerts, and hundreds of artists, both singers and instrumentalists, have appeared on the National Gallery platform in the last six years.

The programmes, designed to last about an hour, were devoted to chamber music of all kinds, instrumental and vocal; and classical music was throughout the mainstay of the repertoire. The composers who drew the largest audiences were, in fact, found to be Beethoven, Mozart and Bach. At the same time British music, old and modern, found a regular place in the programmes, and the catalogue of works performed includes the names of over a hundred British composers. In the classical repertoire a notable feature was the performance of the entire set of Mozart's 21 piano concertos, all the Beethoven quartets and violin and piano sonatas, and the complete chamber works of Brahms. Many of the concerts were broadcast to Home and Overseas listeners, and on several occasions Her Majesty the Queen was present in the audience—notably on the occasion of the 1000th concert on 23rd July 1943. In a tribute paid to Dame Myra Hess, to whose initiative these unique concerts owed their inception, the Director of the National Gallery, speaking on their third anniversary, stressed the importance of the contribution made by Dame Myra in making good music accessible to Londoners during the dreary and dangerous war years. " In all the business and distraction of a complicated enterprise," he said, "Myra Hess has not allowed the highest standards to be relaxed—never in her own playing, and never, so far as is humanly possible, in the choice of artists who play here. To maintain this sense of quality, this feeling that these are standards which must survive all disasters, is the supreme function of the arts in war-time. Those of us who are connected with the Gallery can never be sufficiently grateful for the fact that, through the art of music, it has been able to fulfil in

Dame Myra Hess playing at a war-time National Gallery Concert

The late Edwin Evans

war essentially the same purpose which it fulfilled in peace—that of maintaining through beauty our faith in the greatness of the human spirit." Without that faith it is difficult to see how the country could have survived. The part played by artists and musicians in keeping it alive cannot of course be exactly assessed, but it is certain that their efforts contributed in a very considerable measure to maintaining morale, and keeping alive among ordinary people their appreciation of those spiritual values whose very existence was endangered by the fearful impact of the war.

Sadler's Wells

As can readily be imagined, any kind of operatic enterprise had to contend with even greater handicaps and difficulties than confronted ordinary concert-giving organisations. Opera has never been a really national institution in Britain; the nearest approach to anything of the kind was achieved by the troupe known to the world as the Sadler's Wells Opera who made their home in a theatre built on the site of what was once a famous London theatre called Sadler's Wells. The late Edwin Evans, the well-known critic and writer on music, one-time President of the International Society for Contemporary Music, remarked that, " like so many English musical institutions, with the Promenade Concerts at their head, the Sadler's Wells Opera is difficult to describe because there is so little to which it can be compared. It stands several degrees nearer the Paris *Opéra-Comique* than to the Berlin *Volksoper*, but in reality it has little in common with either of these. It is a modest concern—as yet perhaps too modest to be called a national institution, though most of us look forward to its growing into one after the war. Sadler's Wells, however, has achieved something that more pretentious organisations might well envy: it has achieved singleness of purpose, complete coalescence of artistic effort."

What Sadler's Wells has to offer is, of course, very different from the grand opera which in peace-time used to be presented on a lavish scale, with international star singers and conductors, at Covent Garden. There it was the custom to give operas in their original language, with foreign singers engaged for the occasion from opera-houses all over the world; at Sadler's Wells, on the other hand, they are invariably sung in English, by British artists forming a permanent troupe. And in the years preceding the war this company was firmly established as the only permanent opera company in London, and had built up a repertory of classic and modern operas presented with great care and artistic finish and a team spirit that was wholly admirable. Their policy was progressive: for example it was at Sadler's Wells that the British public was able to see and hear for the first time the authentic original version of " Boris Godounov " in Professor Lamm's edition published by the Soviet State Publishing Co. Another interesting venture was the presentation in the middle of the war of a new and revised staging of Smetana's " The Bartered Bride ". At the second performance the entire theatre was taken by the Czechoslovak Government for the benefit of their soldiers and countrymen, whose delight at seeing an English production of their famous national opera was manifested in scenes of great enthusiasm.

Performances at Sadler's Wells, as in other London theatres, were interrupted when the air raids on the capital began in the autumn of 1940. However, a nucleus of the company was kept in being, and sent off to tour some of the smaller industrial towns not normally visited by touring companies. With an " orchestra " reduced to four, including the conductor at the piano, the entire company numbered only twenty-six; but they defied the difficulties and dangers of travelling about the country and performing in towns which frequently received the unwelcome attentions of the Luftwaffe, and continued cheerfully to present, for example, Mozart's " The Marriage of Figaro " in a *décor* consisting of two chairs and a sofa, Purcell's " Dido and Aeneas ", and some of the favourite operas by Verdi and Puccini.

Before the end of the German war the company returned to London to give seasons from time to time, and as soon as hostilities ceased they settled once more in their original home at Sadler's Wells. It was here in the summer of 1945 that they produced one of the most remarkable operas ever written by a British composer— " Peter Grimes ", by Benjamin Britten, which will be described later in these pages. At the moment of writing, the original Sadler's Wells company has been dissolved, but many of the artists are likely to be merged in a larger venture which will lead ultimately to the foundation for the first time in British musical history of a genuinely " National " Opera.

B.B.C.

Before we close our chapter on the activities, during the war years, of the music-makers—of all those, that is to say, who were engaged in the actual performance or organisation of music, as distinct from the composers (with whom we shall be dealing in the remaining pages of this brochure)—mention should be made of the important services rendered to music by the British Broadcasting Corporation (B.B.C.). The transition from peace to war necessitated a radical readjustment in every department of the B.B.C. which naturally took some time to effect. The initial difficulties, thanks to a pre-arranged plan, were, however, in due course overcome, and, after a rather groping and tentative start, by 1940 the Corporation's music programmes showed a definite improvement. It must not be forgotten that the moment hostilities were declared the broadcasting orchestras and a large proportion of the programme and administrative staffs were evacuated to the country; and at the same time many performers and artists, including orchestral players, were called up or left voluntarily to join one or other of the Forces. The B.B.C. Symphony Orchestra, for example, lost at one stroke thirty of its youngest players on the first day of the war, leaving the remaining ninety to carry on at their first war-time base which was set up at Bristol. There they stayed, with their conductor Sir Adrian Boult, until the summer of 1941. During the previous autumn and winter, Bristol became a target for the Luftwaffe, and the orchestra went through many hair-raising experiences and had many narrow escapes. One musician was killed by a bomb, and the leader of the orchestra, Paul Beard (principal violin), was once blown off his bicycle, though he escaped without serious injury. Sometimes during the bombardment the electricity would fail in the studio and the programme would have to be finished by the light

of candles or oil-lamps.   On one occasion, we are told, the principal violin knelt on the ground beside the microphone in a con-
stricted underground studio to play Bach's " Air on the G String "
while the bombs rained down outside.   How many listeners overseas could ever have guessed under what conditions our artists were
working during those dark days !   And yet broadcasting went on, and
though recorded programmes had sometimes to be substituted for
" live " ones, they invariably went on the air as advertised and at the
appointed time.   In 1941 both the B.B.C. Symphony and Theatre
Orchestras were moved to safer spots, and it was from Bedford, a
small town in the Midlands, that the Symphony Orchestra gave
all its studio broadcasts from that time until the end of the
war.

Practically all the members of the orchestra joined the Home
Guard, which meant that when they were not actually playing or
rehearsing they were attending drills or parades, going on manœuvres
or guarding the studios and broadcasting headquarters with rifles
and fixed bayonets.   Moreover, in addition to its regular broadcasting duties the orchestra, since 1942, undertook a series of tours
in order to play to service men and women in camps and training
centres all over the country, and to factory workers at their jobs.
Among the places visited by the B.B.C. Symphony Orchestra were
R.A.F. and Army camps in Wales and the Midlands, American
camps in the West of England, the important naval centres of Portsmouth and Southampton, and the famous military establishment
Aldershot.   In addition to the more popular classical masterpieces,
for which there was everywhere a great demand, the programmes
included works by such composers as Sibelius, Debussy, Vaughan
Williams, Delius, Elgar and Holst, which were everywhere listened
to with eagerness and real appreciation.   Many stories are told of
the interest aroused among the men and their reactions to hearing
music of this quality played by a first-rate symphony orchestra.
For example, there was that R.A.F. sergeant in Wales who, after
hearing a rehearsal of a Symphony by Sibelius, said he had never had
such a thrill in his life—" I shall be at every concert," he exclaimed;
" I only wish they went on for weeks."   Many of the men who
listened to these concerts in the camps had come to England to

fight from overseas, like that dark-skinned soldier from Jamaica who wanted Sir Adrian Boult's photograph, and in asking for it made the following little speech: " I cannot tell you the pleasure I have had. I come from Jamaica where I used to make music myself. I get little opportunity now in the Army either to make or listen to music. So it has been a privilege today for me—that music and that playing. Thank you, sir, thank you very much." If further proof be needed that good music is appreciated by a far wider public than that which regularly attends concerts, it is on record that in one camp the famous pianist Solomon, in the course of a recital he was giving to the troops, asked his audience what he should play. One half demanded the " Appassionata " sonata of Beethoven, the other half the " Waldstein ". . . . But of course the main work of the B.B.C. Symphony Orchestra and the other broadcasting orchestras, Theatre, Variety, Revue, as well as of the B.B.C. Singers (chorus-master, Leslie Woodgate) and of the many solo artists and chamber music ensembles who appeared regularly before the microphone, was carried on from the studio. From here they broadcast not only to Home listeners, but also to Europe and to America, North and South, India, and all the countries of the British Commonwealth. There was, in fact, scarcely a spot on the globe that did not hear, even during the darkest days of the war, the musical voice of Britain. And in the programmes broadcast, some place was always found for contemporary British music, as the following list of only a few of the many British works, broadcast or performed for the first time by the B.B.C. will show:

William Walton
    Prelude and " Spitfire " Fugue
    Violin Concerto
    Incidental Music to " Macbeth "
    Overture " Scapino ".
    Christopher Columbus

John Ireland
    Epic March
    Three Pastels for Piano
    " These Things Shall Be "

E. J. Moeran
  Violin Concerto
  Rhapsody for Piano and Orchestra

Vaughan Williams
  Symphony No. 5 in D.
  Incidental Music to Bunyan's " Pilgrim's Progress "
  Victory Anthem

Benjamin Britten
  7 Sonnets of Michaelangelo
  Hymn to St. Cecilia
  Sinfonia da Requiem
  A Ceremony of Carols
  " Peter Grimes "

Edmund Rubbra
  Symphony No. 4
  Introduction and Dance

Alan Rawsthorne
  Piano Concerto
  Incidental Music to Red Army programme

Arnold Bax
  Film Music: " Malta, G.C."
  Symphony No. 7 (1st Concert performance in London)
  Violin Concerto
  Legend

Arthur Bliss
  String Quartet

Michael Tippett
  Second String Quartet
  Cantata: " Boyhood's End "
  Oratorio: " A Child of Our Time "

Constant Lambert
  Aubade Héroïque

Lennox Berkeley
  Symphony
  Four Concert Studies

This list does not pretend to include more than a few works by the more important British composers. Among outstanding foreign works broadcast by the B.B.C. may be mentioned: " Symphony in C " and " Apollo Musagetes ", Stravinsky; " Festival Mass ", Janáček; Violin Concerto, Bartók; " Leningrad " and Eighth Symphonies, Shostakovitch; Symphony in E flat, Hindemith; Symphony No. 3, Roy Harris; and works by Honegger, Roussel, Prokofiev, etc. etc.

In 1940 the B.B.C. Symphony Orchestra was conducted by Albert Wolff, who came over from Paris just before the Fall of France; by Gregor Fitelberg from Poland; and by the Belgian conductor Désiré Defauw; and in the winter of 1943 it had the privilege of playing at a public concert under the eminent Portuguese conductor from Lisbon, Pedro de Freitas Branco. This concert was relayed by Emisora Nacional and aroused the greatest interest in both British and Portuguese musical circles. Then in the autumn of 1944, after the liberation of France, musical relations between Britain and France were happily restored, after an interruption of five years, by the visit to this country of such distinguished musicians as Charles Munch and Paul Paray, both of whom conducted the B.B.C. Symphony Orchestra in concerts that were broadcast; while the B.B.C.'s chief conductor, Sir Adrian Boult, went to Paris the following spring to conduct the Orchestre de la Société des Concerts du Conservatoire and the Orchestre National de la Radiodiffusion Française. Francis Poulenc and Pierre Bernac also revisited England, and Poulenc's cantata " Figure Humaine " received its first world performance when it was broadcast, in an English translation, by the B.B.C. Singers, conductor Leslie Woodgate, in March 1945. Among the soloists who came over from Paris to Broadcast for the B.B.C. were Yvonne Lefébure and Nicole Henriot, pianists, and Ginette Neveu, violinist, all of whom had a warm welcome. With the restoration of peace it is to be hoped that a free interchange of artists of all nations will speedily become a reality again, and that British music will find its way to other lands while we in Britain may learn more of what our neighbours have been doing since communications were interrupted by the war.

It is in this field that the British Council has a part to play, and our readers may be interested to hear what the Council's Music Department has accomplished since its inception some ten years ago. One of its principal activities has been the establishment of Music Libraries in various countries abroad where British works are constantly available, either in the form of gramophone records or in print. The largest and best equipped of these libraries, of which there are no less than fifty-seven now functioning in various parts of the world, are at present in Stockholm, Cairo and Buenos Aires. In the Stockholm library alone some seventy-five British composers, both living and dead, are represented. In Portugal, Scandinavia and Latin America especially the keenest interest is taken in British music, while there is scarcely a country, from China to Peru, where the Council has not set up some organisation to render our music accessible, in some form or other, to local amateurs and professional bodies wishing to hear or perform it. Since the formation of the Council's Music Department, for example, no fewer than 500 major works by British composers have been hired and sent abroad. At the same time the Council has made itself responsible for a number of special recordings of outstanding works by British composers which have since been circulated throughout the world.

The list of these includes 98 copies of William Walton's " Belshazzar's Feast ", 88 of the Bliss Piano Concerto, 85 of Moeran's Symphony in G minor, 82 of Bax's Third Symphony, 77 of the Fifth Symphony of Vaughan Williams, and 75 of Holst's " The Hymn of Jesus ". This collection has recently been increased by the addition of the following recordings, specially sponsored by the Council: Elgar's " The Dream of Gerontius "; " The Planets " by Gustav Holst; Purcell's " Dido and Aeneas "; Rawsthorne's " Street Corner "; Bliss's " Phoenix " March.

Many of the records thus disseminated abroad are used by foreign broadcasting stations, and as a result British music is now reaching the ears of hundreds of thousands of people all over the world who might otherwise never have had an opportunity of hearing it. Among radio stations which have been supplied with records, in addition to those in outlying parts of the Empire such as the A.B.C.

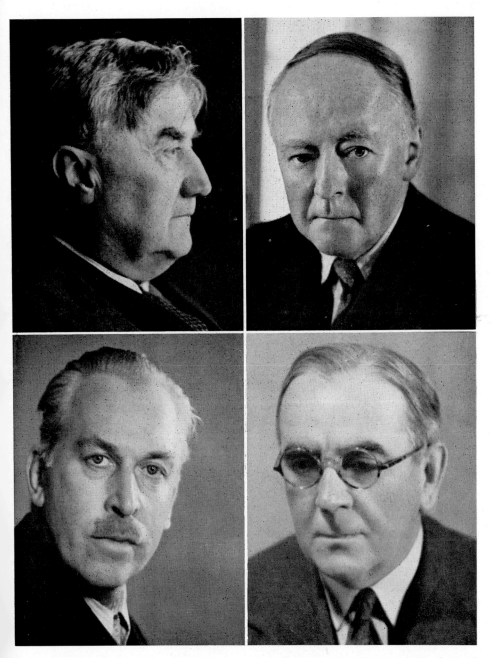

Above: RALPH VAUGHAN WILLIAMS
Below: ARTHUR BLISS

Above: Sir ARNOLD BAX, Master of the King's Musick
Below: JOHN IRELAND

EDMUND RUBBRA (Photo: *Peggy Delius*)

The Huddersfield Choral Society

of Australia and stations in Africa and B.W.I., may be mentioned Radio Provincia, of Buenos Aires; Radio Levant, Syria; the Broadcasting station of Jerusalem, and the Icelandic State Broadcasting Station.

Furthermore, the Council has been instrumental in securing live performances of important British works in many places abroad, so that we read of Purcell's " Golden Sonata " being performed in Argentina and in Mauritius ; of Bliss's " Things to Come " played at three concerts in Bari; and of performances of Britten, Vaughan Williams and Walton in Paris, Palestine, Sweden, Portugal, Trinidad, Chile and Uruguay. And the list could be almost indefinitely extended.

Some of the keenest admirers of British music are to be found in the South American Republics, and three thousand works have been sent to Argentina alone. Russia, too, is taking an increasing interest in our music, there being a great demand for our folk-songs, many of which have been recently arranged by Soviet composers and sung by the Red Army Choir and other choral societies. It is gratifying, too, to be able to record that the 250th anniversary of the death of Purcell was celebrated in March 1946 in Moscow by a performance of " Dido and Aeneas " which took place at the Home of Scientists under the direction of Professor Sadovnikov; while lectures on contemporary British music have been given by Igor Boelza and others. We learn, too, that the great Russian violinist Oistrach is adding to his repertoire Elgar's Violin Concerto.

Before concluding this necessarily brief survey of the British Council's work on behalf of British music and musicians, which includes, of course, giving facilities to British artists enabling them to give concerts in important centres all over the world, mention should be made of one more of the Council's undertakings which was found during the war to be of the greatest value to foreigners desiring to become better acquainted with our music. A Library of Gramophone Records was formed in this country for the benefit of members of foreign missions and Service men and women stationed over here upon which they could draw when arranging programmes in camps, clubs, etc., for their own nationals. The

Council made a point of including at least one British work in every
parcel sent out, and the scheme proved very popular—how popular
may be judged from the fact that from 25 to 30 parcels of records
were dispatched from this library every day.

It may be seen from the above bird's-eye view of what the
British Council has done and is doing for British music that the good
seed already sown has by no means fallen on stony ground.

II. COMPOSERS

As can be readily imagined, the war years were not particularly propitious to composers of serious music in Britain.   The
general disorganisation of life, the material discomfort and dangers
during the periods of sustained air attack, and the mental and
physical strain from which anyone living under these conditions,
and especially artists, were bound to suffer were not, on the whole,
conducive to creative work of any kind.   Nevertheless many of our
leading composers managed to do good work, and in some cases
had the satisfaction of seeing it performed during the war.[1]   Let us
consider, first of all, four of Britain's best-known composers who
are all today over the age of fifty and see what they managed to
produce since 1939.

Sir Arnold Bax (b. 1883) has for long been one of the foremost
figures in British music.   He is also one of the most prolific, count-
ing among his musical " baggage " no less than seven symphonies,
numerous tone-poems, some important choral works, several
concertos, and a substantial body of chamber works, songs and
piano music.   He was knighted in 1937, and in 1942 was made
Master of the King's Music, an ancient Court appointment
which carries with it the duty of supervising the music used at
ceremonial State occasions.   The post was created in the seventeenth
century, in the reign of Charles II, and among the distinguished
musicians who have borne the title since its foundation we find the
names of John Eccles (1650–1735), William Boyce (1710–1799),
Sir Edward Elgar (1857–1934) and Walford Davies (1869–1941).

Bax's output since the war has not been large, but in 1941 he

[1] For works which have been recorded, see Appendix.

was commissioned to write the music for a film picturing the defence of Malta, which has been broadcast as a symphonic item. Mention should be made, too, of two short orchestral works, recently completed, entitled " Legend " and " Work in Progress ", and a sonata for 'cello and piano (" Legend ")—all of which have been performed during the war. Bax has also written an " Ode to Russia " for chorus and orchestra, and a set of " Five Fantasies on Polish Christmas Carols " for treble voice and string orchestra. His very latest published compositions are two works for choir and organ—" Te Deum " and " Nunc Dimittis ".

On the eve of his sixtieth birthday Sir Arnold's Seventh Symphony was broadcast, and on St. Cecilia's Day, 22nd November 1943, his Violin Concerto received its first performance. The soloist was the late Eda Kersey, one of Britain's leading violinists, whose death during the war was a great loss to British music, and the work was broadcast by the B.B.C.

Since 1940 Sir Arnold Bax has been living in a quiet village in the South of England.

The doyen of British composers, Ralph Vaughan Williams (b. 1872), although engaged on war work of various kinds in the country locality where he lives, nevertheless found time to write during the war years several major works. First amongst these must be placed his Fifth Symphony, a truly noble work epitomising in a mood of, for the most part, sustained serenity the accumulated experiences of a long life of single-hearted devotion to the art of music. In a sense the symphony could be described as a synthesis, a summing-up of the composer's musical outlook and aspirations expressed in his own unmistakable idiom, ripened now to a splendid maturity. The Fifth Symphony was broadcast on its first performance at a Promenade Concert in London in the summer of 1943, the composer conducting. Other compositions of note by Vaughan Williams during the period under review include an Oboe Concerto, a String Quartet, and a work for chorus, speaker and orchestra entitled " Thanksgiving for Victory " which was first performed and broadcast on 8th May 1945—the " Victory in Europe " Day which marked the end of the German war.

Vaughan Williams, like many of our younger composers, does

not scorn to write music for the cinema; and among films which have benefited from his distinguished collaboration are " 49th Parallel ", " Coastal Command " and " The Story of a Flemish Farm ". A suite arranged from the latter was performed under the composer's direction at a Promenade Concert in the summer of 1945.

In 1942 Dr. Vaughan Williams celebrated his seventieth birthday, and to mark the occasion a number of British composers wrote works in the form of a tribute to one of the greatest and universally respected figures in contemporary music, and six special concerts were broadcast in his honour.

One of the best-known names among contemporary British composers is that of Arthur Bliss (b. 1891). His early works, which began to appear about 1920, attracted considerable attention. They were provocative, original and full of a most refreshing vitality and unconventionality. Since then his style has greatly matured, although his music is still characterised by these same qualities. His latest works exhibit a remarkable technical proficiency, amounting to a complete command of whatever medium he adopts, and a dynamic rhythmic vitality, combined with a directness of approach, free from any suspicion of insincerity or misplaced emotionalism, from which emerges the impression of an arresting, fully equipped musical personality who has something to say and knows exactly how to say it. When the war broke out Bliss was in America, having been appointed Professor of Music at the University of California. In 1941, however, in response to an invitation from the B.B.C., he returned to England to become, firstly, Assistant Director of Overseas Music, and then Director of Music in the Corporation—a post which he resigned in 1944.

His most important compositions during this period have been the ballets " Miracle in the Gorbals " and " Adam Zero ", both produced by the Sadler's Wells Ballet Company, and the music for two films—" Men of Two Worlds " and " La France Combattante ". His march " The Phoenix ", in honour of France, has been performed in Paris under Charles Munch, since the liberation, and recently recorded.

Finally, mention should be made of his " Seven American Poems " for voice and piano, and a fine String Quartet composed before he

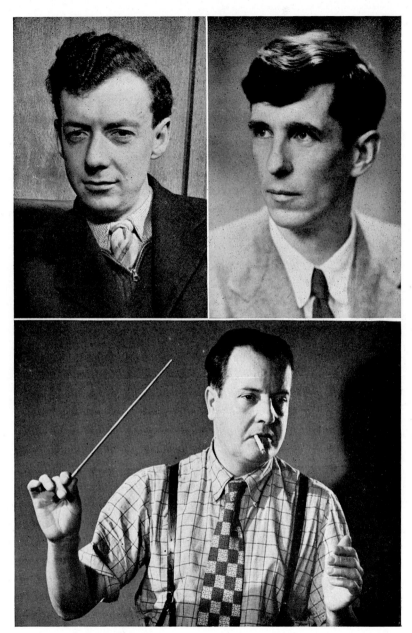

BENJAMIN BRITTEN   MICHAEL TIPPETT
CONSTANT LAMBERT

A scene from Benjamin Britten's opera "Peter Grimes": Peter Pears as Peter Grimes, Joan Cross as Ellen Orford, Leonard Thompson as the Apprentice Boy

(Photo: *Peggy Delius*)

left California at the invitation of Mrs. Elizabeth Sprague Coolidge, and first performed at the University of California in 1941 by the Pro Arte Quartet. In England this has been played and recorded by the Griller Quartet.

The music of William Walton (b. 1902) is probably better known abroad than that of almost any other living British composer. His Symphony, his Concertos for Violin and for Viola, his suite "Façade", the overtures "Portsmouth Point" and "Scapino" and the big choral work "Belshazzar's Feast" are among his best-known works and have made him an outstanding figure in contemporary British music.

The Violin Concerto, completed just before the war, had its first performance in Cleveland, U.S.A., in December 1939, with Heifetz as soloist; and "Scapino", written for the Chicago Symphony Orchestra's fiftieth anniversary, was completed in 1940 and performed there the following year. Other works of this period were "Music for Children", the ballet "The Wise Virgins" (orchestration of music by Bach), and music for the film "Major Barbara" (Bernard Shaw).

The greater part of Walton's output during the war was, at the behest of the Ministry of Labour and National Service, confined to films, to be produced under the auspices of either the War Office or the Ministry of Information. Chief among these must be counted "Next of Kin", "The First of the Few" (dealing with the life of the inventor of the Spitfire) and, last but not least, Shakespeare's "Henry V", the film which provided the major cinematographic sensation of the year 1944. In 1943, however, Walton was able to find time, apart from his official duties, to write the music for a ballet "The Quest", and the incidental music for John Gielgud's production of "Macbeth".

Another composer of note who has had to combine music with military service is Edmund Rubbra (b. 1901), who, as a sergeant in the British Army of Liberation in Germany, was until recently in charge of the Army Music Group. The object of the Music Group, which includes several performers of note, is to give the troops an opportunity of hearing the very best chamber music. These musicians in battle-dress have undertaken tours of camps and train-

C

ing centres in England and Scotland, and are now doing the same in Germany, playing for the Army of Occupation.

Rubbra has written four notable Symphonies, the last of which was completed during the war and first performed at a Promenade Concert in London in 1942. His more recent works include a " Soliloquy " (for solo 'cello, string orchestra, 2 horns and tympani) and a " Mass " for double choir which was commissioned by Canterbury Cathedral. Rubbra's music is original without being eccentric in any way: in the words of a contemporary critic, " he reaches out to new fields of expression while keeping one foot in the ancient ways ". One of the best and most attractive of his chamber works is the Second Violin and Piano Sonata; while his " Sinfonia Concertante ", for piano and orchestra, revised and performed since the war, with the composer playing the solo part, must be counted as one of his major works.

John Ireland (b. 1879) was another of the pioneers of the British musical revival which set in about the beginning of the twentieth century, and his compositions have greatly enriched the modern repertoire. His piano and chamber music rank high in the estimation of the best critics; among his major works may be cited the Concerto for Piano and Orchestra, and the big choral work " These Things Shall Be ". When war broke out, Ireland was living in the Channel Islands, on the island of Guernsey, but managed to escape in June 1940 shortly before the German occupation. He brought with him the unfinished sketch of his piano work entitled " Sarnia: an Island Sequence " (Sarnia being the old Roman name for Guernsey), which he completed the following year. This has been performed and broadcast a number of times, as has also the " Epic March " for full orchestra which was commissioned by the B.B.C. Other works dating from this period include a setting of the Morning and Evening Canticles of the Anglican Church, and a set of pieces for the piano entitled " Three Pastels ". Later works include a Fantasy-Sonata for clarinet and piano, and a " Maritime Overture " for Military Band. Ireland also wrote some smaller vocal pieces, including one for treble voices and piano entitled " Ex ore Innocentium ". The composer tells us that none of the above works can be said to be in any way connected with the war, with the possible exception of the "Epic March", which might be taken to suggest some opposition to Nazism and Fascism.

Coming now to the younger generation, we find a number of most talented composers of whom perhaps the most prominent at the present time is Benjamin Britten (b. 1913). Britten's rise to fame has been rapid, following a brilliantly precocious youthful period during which he produced works exhibiting an astonishing technical facility which at one time threatened to outstrip the quality of his musical thought. In his latest works, however, that danger has been dispelled and his art is developing in a way that seems to justify the highest hopes. One of his earliest works to attract the attention of musicians outside his native country was the Quartet for Oboe and Strings performed in 1934 at the Florence Festival of the I.S.C.M. Britten was then aged twenty-one. Then came the "Variations on a Theme of Frank Bridge" which gained for him in 1928 an international reputation. (Frank Bridge, who died in 1940 was a British composer of note who gave Britten his first serious musical instruction and remained his adviser and friend until his death; later Britten studied composition at the Royal College of Music in London under John Ireland.) Among his best-known later works are the "Sinfonia da Requiem" (first performed in New York under Barbirolli in 1941), the First String Quartet, the "Sonnets of Michelangelo" for tenor and piano; the song-cycle "Les Illuminations" (a setting of words by Rimbaud) and the "Serenade" for tenor, horn and strings. The first four of these works were composed or completed in America, where Britten remained from 1939 to 1942; the "Serenade", one of his finest achievements to date, was written after his return to England. His war-time and post-war output also includes three choral works: "Hymn to St. Cecilia" for mixed voices *a cappella*, to words written by the poet W. H. Auden; "A Ceremony of Carols", for treble voices and harp or piano; a festival cantata, "Rejoice in the Lamb", for mixed voices and organ, and the Second String Quartet.

All the above-mentioned works are published and have been performed in the U.S.A., in England and on the continent of Europe.

But perhaps the most outstanding of all his works to date is the opera " Peter Grimes ", which was first produced in London by the Sadler's Wells Opera Company in June 1945. Composed to a libretto by Montagu Slater after the poem by the eighteenth-century " realist " English poet George Crabbe, the opera provides a musical background to a story of a somewhat uncompromising realism in which the protagonist is a sadist fisherman, Peter Grimes, whose brutalities towards the workhouse boys who become his apprentices arouse the anger and indignation of his fellow villagers, who finally drive Grimes to commit suicide. This he does by putting out to sea in his boat and scuttling it. The action takes place in a seaside village on the East Coast of England in and around the market square and tavern; and into the tragic events of the story are woven the changing moods of the sea and the violent emotional reactions of the villagers towards the man whom they feel to be a monster, but into whose spiritual loneliness (the cause of his excesses) they are unable to penetrate. For Grimes is a dual personality—and to suggest this has been one of the composer's main objectives. The opera abounds in moments of extraordinary power and poignancy, and the choral writing, expressing the collective soul of the little township, is no less remarkable than the solo declamatory parts assigned to the chief actors, and the rich and subtle orchestral score which contributes so largely to the opera's overwhelming effect upon the spectator. The orchestral Interludes from the opera have been arranged for concert performance as a Suite, and can be performed separately. " Peter Grimes " is probably Britten's finest achievement to date, and has aroused great interest among both musicians and the general public, who evidently found the work to its liking. The first performance on the Continent of this striking new British opera took place at Stockholm in March 1946, and this was followed, in the same year, by performances at Basle, Zürich, Antwerp and Boston, U.S.A.[1]

It should be added that Britten is a brilliant pianist and, in addition to composing, devotes much of his time to performing, appearing frequently as either solo pianist, accompanist or conductor.

---

[1] A more recent " chamber opera ", with an orchestra of only eleven instruments and percussion, on the story of " The Rape of Lucretia ", had its first performance in England in 1946.

Above: WILLIAM WALTON
Below: ALAN RAWSTHORNE

Above: MALCOLM SARGENT
Below: ELIZABETH LUTYENS

(Photo: *Vogue*)

Yehudi Menuhin

Rehearsal of the Boyd Neel String Orchestra

He very often partners the tenor Peter Pears, who, besides singing Britten's songs, played the part of Peter Grimes in the opera.

It was for Britten and Pears that Michael Tippett (b. 1905), another composer who is now making a name for himself, wrote in 1943 his cantata for tenor and piano, " Boyhood's End ". The cantata was broadcast in 1945, and the composer considers it to be one of his most representative works. Tippett is now Director of Music at Morley College, in South London, an institution which caters for students drawn from the working and professional classes—where music is a prominent feature of the curriculum. The College building was badly damaged by a land-mine in 1940, but work goes on, and the concerts given there are attended by an enthusiastic group of young people, professionals and amateurs. When the war broke out Tippett was working on his " Fantasia for Piano and Orchestra on a Theme of Handel ", and had written the words of his oratorio " A Child of Our Time ", which is one of his major works. This was completed in the spring of 1941, and produced three years later in London. The " hero " of this oratorio, which presents many unfamiliar features—for example some of the choruses take the form of " Negro Spirituals "—was the Polish Jew, Grynspan, who assassinated an official at the German Embassy in Paris in 1938. The work had considerable success, and has since been performed outside London and broadcast by the B.B.C. It has also been broadcast from Brussels. During the war it was performed in London at a concert organised by the Polish Government in aid of their orphans. Other important works of Tippett are his Second String Quartet (produced in 1943) and the Concerto for Double String Orchestra. His most recent works are his Symphony No. 2, which had its *première* at a concert given by the Liverpool Philharmonic Society in November 1945, and the Third String Quartet.

Tippett cultivates a certain austerity of style, and his music tends in the main to be contrapuntal and polyphonic, though by no means devoid of emotional intensity. In the words of a contemporary critic, " he is the only considerable composer I call to mind who has somehow managed to by-pass the nineteenth century—at all events as exhibited in its most characteristic features. His contemporaneity, therefore, rests partly on the revival of musical textures and idioms that recall those of the second half of the sixteenth century, and partly on a certain ' prophetic ' quality which is as difficult to pin down as Britten's medievalism, but which disengages itself powerfully in the experience of listening to his music.   Michael Tippett, even more essentially perhaps than Britten, belongs to the future of music."

Another young composer who is attracting a good deal of attention today is Alan Rawsthorne (b. 1905).   His very great gifts did not reveal themselves to the outside world until he was over thirty (he did not begin to study music seriously until he was twenty), when a work of his was performed at the London Festival of the International Society for Contemporary Music.   This was the " Theme and Variations " for two violins; at the next Festival, held in Warsaw just before war broke out, there was a first performance of his " Symphonic Studies " for orchestra, a strikingly original and characteristic work, revealing the composer's grasp of form and the conciseness of his musical thinking.   Among his writings for the piano the " Bagatelles " are probably the best known, but his finest achievement to date is the Concerto for Piano and Orchestra—a work which has already been heard in Paris and is establishing itself in the repertoire of leading pianists of the day.   During the war Rawsthorne was in uniform and his musical activities were practically confined to writing music for Army Films—a task which he accomplished with the greatest proficiency and brilliance.   He managed to find time, however, outside his military duties, to write an orchestral piece, " Cortèges ", which had its *première* at a Promenade Concert in London in 1945, and to re-score the Piano Concerto—which he did very largely while working in the Quarter-Master's office!   He also has in preparation a Concerto for Violin, the original MS. of which was destroyed when his flat was hit by a bomb during the London " blitz ", and has recently completed an overture for E.N.S.A. entitled " Street Corner ".   In the meantime musicians everywhere will be awaiting with eagerness the next work from his pen, for Rawsthorne is a composer who will undoubtedly make his mark.

The same remark applies, one feels, to Lennox Berkeley (b. 1903), who received the major part of his musical training in Paris from the celebrated French composer, conductor and teacher, Mlle. Nadia Boulanger. Berkeley's music has an unmistakable Gallic flavour, as might be expected in view of his training and residence in Paris for a period of over six years ; but in his most recent works his personality is establishing itself more firmly while his style matures. Berkeley has written a good deal of music since 1939, in spite of having been on the staff of the B.B.C. since 1942. His orchestral works include a Symphony, which has been performed at a " Prom " in London, with the composer conducting; a " Divertimento " (commissioned by the B.B.C.); and music for two films: " Hotel Reserve " and " Out of Chaos ". He has also been particularly active in the field of chamber music, having written a String Trio, Second String Quartet, a Sonatina for Violin and Piano, a Sonata for Viola and Piano, and a Sonata for Piano Solo. Previous to the war he had written an oratorio, " Jonah " (broadcast in 1936), and music for a ballet, " The Judgment of Paris ", produced at Sadler's Wells in 1938. He has also had works performed at Festivals of the I.S.C.M. in Barcelona and London.

The name of Constant Lambert (b. 1905) is familiar to musicians both in and outside Britain on account of his great versatility as composer, conductor and author of one of the best books on modern music, *Music Ho !* Lambert's name first came before the international public in 1926 when his ballet " Romeo and Juliet ", which had been commissioned by Diaghilev, was performed by the Russian Ballet at Monte Carlo. Three years later came " The Rio Grande " for solo piano, chorus and orchestra on a poem by Sacheverell Sitwell which still remains one of his most characteristic works. His masterpiece, however, is probably the Masque for Orchestra, Chorus and Baritone Solo, with words by the Elizabethan poet Thomas Nashe, entitled " Summer's Last Will and Testament ". This is a thoroughly mature, finely balanced and imaginatively conceived work which shows the composer at the height of his powers. For some years now Lambert has devoted a large part of his time to conducting and is now musical director and chief conductor of the Sadler's Wells Ballet, which is a great feature of London life. He has himself written two ballets—" Horoscope " and " Pomona ", but since the war he has done more conducting than composing. In 1940 he was in Holland touring with the Sadler's Wells Ballet Company when the German invasion of the Netherlands was launched, but managed to escape with all the other artists in the nick of time. As it was they had to leave behind much of their valuable scenery and stage property. This experience inspired Lambert to write his " Aubade Héroïque " for orchestra, the idea of which came to him while he was standing on the quay at Rotterdam, waiting for the boat to take him back to England, and watching the sun rise over the Dutch landscape. Another of Lambert's wartime compositions takes the form of an orchestral suite from the music he wrote for a film called " Merchant Seamen ".

Constant Lambert has often appeared as a conductor on the Continent—for example he conducted William Walton's " Belshazzar's Feast " at the I.S.C.M. Festival in Amsterdam in 1933, and in 1937 he went with the Sadler's Wells Ballet to Paris to conduct the special performances they gave at the Exhibition. He was in Paris again in the spring of 1945 when the ballet appeared at the Théâtre des Champs-Élysées. Later in the year he made his first appearance as Associate Conductor of the London Promenade Concerts, sharing duties with Sir Adrian Boult and Mr. Basil Cameron.

E. J. Moeran (b. 1894) is a composer who has increased his output considerably since the war, having produced a Violin Concerto (1942), a Rhapsody for Piano and Orchestra (1943), an " Overture to a Masque " (1944), a " Sinfonietta " (1944) and a Concerto for Violoncello and Orchestra (1945). His music is refreshingly free from pretension, and is the reflection of a musical personality drawing its inspiration from nature and sensitive to the appeal of the folk element in the music of his native land.

Our gallery of musicians would not be complete without some mention of the composer Patrick Hadley (b. 1899) who is a Doctor of Music at Cambridge University, where he is now Lecturer in Music and Fellow of Gonville and Caius College. Most of Hadley's compositions are choral, one of his most important being a Symphony of three orchestral movements with a vocal finale entitled " The Trees so High ". This is scored for large orchestra with baritone solo and mixed chorus. Since the war he has been, as he expresses it, "engrossed in helping to keep the musical flag flying in Cambridge", where besides lecturing he took over the duties of conductor of the Cambridge University Musical Society. Performances under his *bâton* included Beethoven's "Mass in D", the Mozart "Requiem", the Brahms Violin Concerto, "Appalachia" and "Song of the High Hills" by Delius, and the first performance of his own latest important work, "Travellers". This was written during the war, and is dedicated to the men who left Cambridge to serve their country. This has been broadcast, and was performed at a Promenade Concert in London in the summer of 1945. Another large-scale work from his pen may be expected soon, for chorus, orchestra and eight soloists. This is called "The Hills" and is in the press at the time of writing. Hadley is a sensitive musician with a great feeling for the English language and the English landscape, and occasionally makes effective use of folk idiom.

The musical Renaissance in Britain, so noticeable since the turn of the century, has been marked by the advent of several women composers whose works command attention. A pioneer in this field was the late Dame Ethel Smyth (1858-1944), who wrote among other things several operas, the best known of which are "The Wreckers" and "The Boatswain's Mate", and who by her example undoubtedly inspired many women to apply themselves to the difficult art of composition. Of the present generation two British women composers at least have succeeded in making a name for themselves—Elizabeth Lutyens and Elizabeth Maconchy. Miss Lutyens, who is now the wife of that very well-known student and promoter of contemporary music, Edward Clark, was particularly active during the war and produced a number of works which undoubtedly add to her already growing reputation as a composer with a style of her own and a very definite musical personality. It so happened that her "Three Pieces for Orchestra" were played at a Promenade Concert conducted by the late Sir Henry Wood on the night when the Germans opened their air offensive against London. The following year she was evacuated with her children to the country, where in the face of all sorts of difficulties and in the intervals of looking after her husband

and family she managed nevertheless to compose a number of works, one of which, the " Concerto for Nine Instruments ", was accepted by the English Jury of the I.S.C.M. in 1940 and has been performed both in London and in the U.S.A.   Among other recent works from her pen are the " Nine Bagatelles " for 'cello and piano; a Concerto for Clarinet, Saxophone, Piano and String Orchestra; " Five Intermezzi " for piano solo, and " Three Salutes to the United Nations ".   Since returning to London Miss Lutyens has written " Three Symphonic Preludes " for orchestra, performed at the Festival of the I.S.C.M. in London in July 1946; an overture, " Proud City " (in honour of London); a Concerto for Bassoon and String Orchestra; some film music; and a " Suite Gauloise ", the first movement of which was commissioned by the French Government for inclusion in an album of piano pieces by British composers entitled " Hommage à la France ".   Mention should also be made of a striking Sonata for Solo Viola which had its first performance at a concert organised by the Society for the Promotion of New Music.

Elizabeth Maconchy (b. 1907) is, like Miss Lutyens, a modernist and cultivates a style that has been described by a contemporary critic as " vigorous and thoughtful, sometimes impassioned but rarely lyrical ".   Her music has on several occasions found favour with the Juries of the I.S.C.M. and several of her works have been performed on the Continent, notably at Brussels, Warsaw, Prague, Budapest and Cracow.   Of Irish parentage, but largely trained and mostly resident in England, Elizabeth Maconchy started to compose at the age of six.   She has written four String Quartets, an Oboe Quintet, a Concerto for Viola and Orchestra, and a Piano Concerto which was performed in Prague in 1930.

When war broke out Miss Maconchy was living in Southern England, and while the Battle of Britain was proceeding overhead she wrote her ballet " Puck Fair ", which was produced in Dublin at the Gaiety Theatre the same year (1940).   Her " Dialogue for Piano and Orchestra " was to have had its first performance at a Promenade Concert the same year, but owing to air raids the concerts had to be discontinued.   However, the work was given two years later under the late Sir Henry Wood, with Clifford Curzon as the soloist.   More recent works from her pen include: String Quartet

No. 4 (broadcast by the B.B.C. in their Home and Foreign Services); a set of Variations for Orchestra, commissioned by the B.B.C. and broadcast in the special programmes to celebrate the seventieth birthday of Vaughan Williams; Variations for String Orchestra (broadcast from Dublin in July 1945); a Sonata for Violin and Piano (performed at a concert of the London Contemporary Music Society in 1945); and several songs and smaller works. To this period also belongs a choral work, for women's voices, entitled " Stalingrad ", which has been performed in London and at Music Festivals in the provinces. Miss Maconchy's Concertino for Clarinet and Strings has been selected for performance at I.S.C.M. Festival at Copenhagen in June 1947.

It is time now to close this brief survey of the activities and achievements of British musicians during the war. Enough has perhaps been said to provide evidence that, in spite of the material dangers and difficulties to which this country was exposed during six long years, spiritual and artistic values were never lost sight of or allowed to be submerged in the heat and dust of the struggle. Musically, Britain has won her spurs and can now face the future with confidence. Gone are the days when it was possible for foreign nations to refer to her as " the land without music ". It was never true, and never less so than today.

APPENDIX

GRAMOPHONE RECORDS

* Specially recorded under the auspices of the British Council.

Arnold Bax

" A Hill Tune "; " A Mountain Mood ". Harriet Cohen (Pianoforte). COL. DX.1109.

" Hardanger " (Sonata for Two Pianos). Ethel Bartlett and Rae Robertson (Pianofortes). N.G.S. 156-8.

" Tintagel "; " Mediterranean ". New Symphony Orchestra conducted by Eugene Goossens. H.M.V. C.1619-20.

Oboe Quintet. Leon Goossens (Oboe) and the International String Quartet. N.G.S. 76-7.

Overture to a Picaresque Comedy. London Philharmonic Orchestra conducted by Sir Hamilton Harty. COL. LX.394.

Sonata for Viola and Harp. Watson Forbes (Viola) and Maria Korchinska (Harp). DECCA K.941-3.

String Quartet in G Major No. 1. Marie Wilson String Quartet. N.G.S. 153-5.

String Quartet in G Major No. 1. The Griller Quartet. DECCA K.1009-12.

Symphony No. 3.* Hallé Orchestra conducted by John Barbirolli. H.M.V. C.3380-5 (Non-Automatic). H.M.V. C. 7593-8 (Automatic).

English Music Society, Vol. 2 :

Sonata for Viola and Piano; Nonett for String Quartet, with Bass, Flute, Clarinet, Oboe and Harp; Mater Ora Filium. William Primrose (Viola), Harriet Cohen (Pianoforte), Griller String Quartet, Leon Goossens (Oboe), Frederick Thurston (Clarinet), Jos. Slater (Flute), Victor Watson (Bass), Maria Korchinska (Harp), B.B.C. Chorus conducted by Leslie Woodgate. COL. ROX.179-85 (Non-Automatic). COL. ROX.8039-45 (Automatic).

" I Heard a Piper Piping "; Linden Lea (Vaughan Williams). Astra Desmond (Contralto) and Gerald Moore (Pianoforte). DECCA M.522.

Arthur Bliss

Clarinet Quintet; Polonaise. Frederick Thurston (Clarinet) and Griller String Quartet. DECCA K.780-3.

Concerto for Pianoforte and Orchestra.* Solomon (Pianoforte) and Liverpool Philharmonic Orchestra conducted by Sir Adrian Boult.

A famous English musical family—Sidonie and Marie Goossens, harpists of the B.B.C and London Symphony Orchestras, Eugene, composer-conductor, and Leon, solo oboist

The new home of the " Proms " : the Royal Albert Hall

H.M.V. C.3348-52 (Non-Automatic). H.M.V. C.7583-7 (Automatic).

Film Music ("Things to Come"). London Symphony Orchestra. DECCA K.810-11 and K.817.

Music for Strings. B.B.C. Symphony Orchestra conducted by Sir Adrian Boult. H.M.V. DB.3257-9 (Non-Automatic). H.M.V. DB.8342-4 (Automatic).

Quartet in B Flat. Griller String Quartet. DECCA K.1091-4.

Sonata for Viola and Piano. Watson Forbes (Viola) and Myers Foggin (Pianoforte). DECCA X.233-5.

"Baraza" (Incidental music from the film "Men of Two Worlds"). Eileen Joyce (Pianoforte) and the National Symphony Orchestra and Male Chorus conducted by Muir Mathieson. DECCA K.1174.

The Phoenix March* (in honour of France). Philharmonia Orchestra conducted by Constant Lambert. H.M.V. C.3518.

"Miracle in the Gorbals"—Ballet Suite. Royal Opera House Orchestra, Covent Garden, conducted by Constant Lambert. COL. DX.1260-61.

Benjamin Britten

Introduction and Rondo alla Burlesca for Two Pianos, Opus 23, No. 1. Clifford Curzon and Benjamin Britten. DECCA K.1117.

Mazurka Elegiaca for Two Pianos, Opus 23, No. 2. Clifford Curzon and Benjamin Britten. DECCA K.1118.

"Le Roi s'en va-t-en chasse"; "La Belle est au Jardin d'Amour" (French Folk Songs). Sophie Wyss (Soprano) and Benjamin Britten (Pianoforte). DECCA M.568.

Seven Sonnets of Michelangelo, Nos. XXX, XVI and XXXI (in Italian). Peter Pears (Tenor) and Benjamin Britten (Pianoforte). H.M.V. B.9302 and H.M.V. C.3312.

Simple Symphony. Boyd Neel String Orchestra conducted by Boyd Neel. DECCA X.245-7.

Variations on a Theme of Frank Bridge. Boyd Neel String Orchestra conducted by Boyd Neel. DECCA X.226-8.

Serenade for Tenor, Horn and Strings. Peter Pears (Tenor), Dennis Brain (Horn) and the Boyd Neel String Orchestra conducted by Benjamin Britten. DECCA K.1151-3 (Non-Automatic). DECCA AK.1151-3 (Automatic).

A Ceremony of Carols. The Morriston Boys' Choir with Maria Korchinska (Harp). Choir Master: Ivor Sims. DECCA K.1155-7 (Non-Automatic). DECCA AK.1155-7 (Automatic).

Hymn to St. Cecilia, Opus 27; "This have I done", Opus 34 (Holst). Fleet Street Choir conducted by T. B. Lawrence. DECCA K.1088-9.

Folk Songs: "The Sally Gardens", "Little Sir William" and "Oliver Cromwell". Peter Pears (Tenor) and Benjamin Britten (Pianoforte). DECCA M.555.

John Ireland

Concerto in E Flat for Pianoforte and Orchestra. Eileen Joyce (Pianoforte) and the Hallé Orchestra conducted by Leslie Heward. COL. DX.1072-4 (Non-Automatic). COL. DX.8178-80 (Automatic).

Concertino Pastorale; Downland Suite (Minuet). Boyd Neel String Orchestra conducted by Boyd Neel. DECCA X.253-5.

Phantasie Trio in A Minor; Holy Boy. Grinke Trio. DECCA K.899-900.

Trio No. 3 in E. Grinke Trio. DECCA X.242-4.

London Overture. Liverpool Philharmonic Orchestra conducted by Dr. Malcolm Sargent. COL. DX.1155-6.

"Sea Fever"; "The Road to the Isles" (Kennedy-Fraser). Robert Irwin (Baritone). H.M.V. B.9073.

"Sea Fever"; "Absent" (Metcalfe). Paul Robeson (Bass). H.M.V. B.9257.

Constant Lambert

Horoscope—Ballet Suite. Liverpool Philharmonic Orchestra conducted by Constant Lambert. COL. DX.1196-7.

E. J. Moeran

Symphony in G Minor.* The Hallé Orchestra conducted by Leslie Heward. H.M.V. C.3319-24 (Non-Automatic). H.M.V. C.7566-71 (Automatic).

Alan Rawsthorne

"Street Corner" Overture.* Philharmonia Orchestra conducted by Constant Lambert. H.M.V. C.3502.

Bagatelles for Piano. Four (1938). Denis Matthews. H.M.V. C. 3324.

Ralph Vaughan Williams

Concerto Accademico (Concerto in D minor for Violin and String Orchestra). Frederick Grinke (Violin) and Boyd Neel String Orchestra conducted by Boyd Neel. DECCA X.248-9.

English Folk Songs (Suite). Columbia Broadcasting Symphony Orchestra. COL. DB.1930-31.

Greensleeves Fantasia. Hallé Orchestra conducted by Dr. Malcolm Sargent. COL. DX.1087.

Fantasia on a Theme by Thomas Tallis. B.B.C. Symphony Orchestra conducted by Sir Adrian Boult. H.M.V. DB.3958-9.

" The Lark Ascending "; " Eventide ". Frederick Grinke (Violin) and Boyd Neel Orchestra conducted by Boyd Neel. DECCA X.259-60.

" Serenade to Music." B.B.C. Orchestra with Sixteen Famous Soloists conducted by Sir Henry Wood. COL. LX.757-8.

Symphony in F Minor (No. 4.). B.B.C. Symphony Orchestra conducted by Dr. Ralph Vaughan Williams. H.M.V. DB.3367-70 (Non-Automatic). H.M.V. DB.8406-9 (Automatic).

Symphony in D Major* (No. 5). Hallé Orchestra conducted by John Barbirolli. H.M.V. C.3388-92 (Non-Automatic). H.M.V. C.7599-603 (Automatic).

" The Wasps " Overture; Fantasia on " Greensleeves " (Vaughan Williams). Queen's Hall Orchestra conducted by Sir Henry Wood. DECCA K.821-2.

" A London Symphony." Queen's Hall Orchestra conducted by Sir Henry Wood. DECCA X.114-18.

" The Wasps " Overture. Hallé Orchestra conducted by Dr. Malcolm Sargent. COL. DX. 1088.

" Linden Lea "; " I Heard a Piper Piping " (Bax). Astra Desmond (Contralto) and Gerald Moore (Pianoforte). DECCA M.522.

Job—A Masque for Dancing. B.B.C. Symphony Orchestra conducted by Sir Adrian Boult. H.M.V. DB.6289-94 (Non-Automatic). H.M.V. DB.9024-8 (Automatic).

" Silent Noon "; " Tell me Ye Flowerets " (Stanford). David Lloyd (Tenor). COL. DB.2159.

William Walton

" Belshazzar's Feast."* Liverpool Philharmonic Orchestra and Brass Bands, Dennis Noble (Baritone) and the Huddersfield Choir conducted by Dr. William Walton. H.M.V. C.3330-34 (Non-Automatic). H.M.V. C.7572-6 (Automatic).

Concerto for Viola and Orchestra. Frederick Riddle (Viola) and the London Symphony Orchestra conducted by Dr. William Walton. DECCA X.199-201.

Concerto for Violin and Orchestra. Jascha Heifetz (Violin) and Cincinnati Symphony Orchestra conducted by Eugene Goossens. H.M.V. DB.5953-5 (Non-Automatic). H.M.V. DB.8911-13 (Automatic).

" Crown Imperial "—Coronation March, 1937. B.B.C. Symphony Orchestra with Berkeley Mason (Organ) conducted by Sir Adrian Boult. H.M.V. DB.3164.

"Façade" Suite No. 1. London Philharmonic Orchestra conducted by Dr. William Walton. H.M.V. C.2836-7.

"Façade" Suite No. 2; Siesta. London Philharmonic Orchestra conducted by Dr. William Walton. H.M.V. C.3042.

Piano Quartet. Reginald Paul Piano Quartet. DECCA X.2238-41.

"Portsmouth Point" Overture. B.B.C. Symphony Orchestra conducted by Sir Adrian Boult. H.M.V. DA.1540.

Prelude and "Spitfire" Fugue. Hallé Orchestra conducted by Dr. William Walton. H.M.V. C.3359.

"Scapino"—A Comedy Overture. Chicago Symphony Orchestra.

Symphony in B Flat Minor. London Symphony Orchestra conducted by Sir Hamilton Harty. DECCA X.108-13.

"Wise Virgins" Ballet Suite. Sadler's Wells Orchestra conducted by Dr. William Walton. H.M.V. C.3178-9.

"Sinfonia Concertante"; "Death of Falstaff"; "Touch her Lips". Phyllis Sellick (Pianoforte) and City of Birmingham Orchestra conducted by Dr. William Walton ("Sinfonia Concertante"). Philharmonia Orchestra conducted by Dr. William Walton ("Death of Falstaff" and "Touch her Lips"). H.M.V. C.3478-80 (Non-Automatic). H.M.V. C.7635-7 (Automatic).

"Where does the uttered music go?" B.B.C. Chorus conducted by Leslic Woodgate. H.M.V. C.3503.

Viola Concerto. William Primrose (Viola) and the Philharmonia Orchestra conducted by Dr. William Walton. H.M.V. DB.6309-11. (Non-Automatic). H.M.V. DB.9036-8 (Automatic).